# A Study Of Luther's Small Catechism

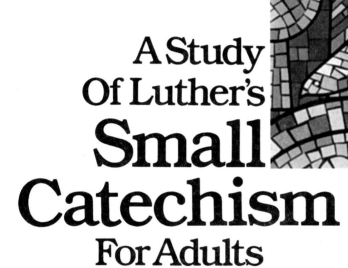

## For Adults

# by Todd Nichol

Augsburg Fortress
Minneapolis

# A Study
# Of Luther's
# Small
# Catechism
## For Adults

**A STUDY OF LUTHER'S SMALL CATECHISM
FOR ADULTS**
Lutheran Faith and Life Series
Adult Study Book

This Student Book is accompanied by a Leader Guide.

Thomas S. Hanson and Carolyn F. Lystig, editors
RUDD,*here!*, inside design
Steve Carlson, illustrations
Gary Baune/Hetland, Ltd., cover artwork, 1, 2, 5, 7, 47
Photos: Robert Fried, 8, 62; Jean S. Buldain, 12, 53;
    Jim Whitmer, 21, 26, 45; K. B. Getz, 32; D. Jeanene
    Tiner, 36; Positive Images/Patricia Sgrignoli, 38;
    Steve Gravano, 56; Nancy Coates, 61.
Koechel Peterson and Associates, Inc., logo and cover
    design

Scripture quotations are from the New Revised
Standard Version Bible, copyright © 1989, Division of
Christian Education of the National Council of
Churches of Christ in the United States of America.
Used by permission.

Manufactured in U.S.A.

Catechism quotations are
from *The Small Catechism by
Martin Luther in
Contemporary English with
Lutheran Book of Worship
Texts (1979 Edition)* copyright
© 1960, 1968.

Quotations identified as *BC*
are from *The Book of Concord*
translated and edited by
Theodore G. Tappert.
Copyright © 1959 Fortress
Press.

Quotations identified as *LW*
are from *Luther's Works*, Vol.
35 © 1960, Vol. 41 © 1966
Fortress Press.

Materials identified as *LBW*
are from *Lutheran Book of
Worship*, copyright © 1978.

# Introduction
## To The Small Catechism

**The notion that it is important** to get back to the basics is nothing new for Christians. That is why centuries ago they invented the idea of the catechism. A catechism is a guide for people in need of instruction—novices and veterans, the young and the old alike—in the fundamentals of Christian faith. In the earliest centuries, Christians used these manuals to prepare new believers for Baptism. As time passed, books of this kind were also prepared for the instruction of baptized believers, too.

**Among Lutherans,** the best known of these summaries of the Christian faith is the Small Catechism by Martin Luther. Although primarily a guide to Christian essentials for ordinary Christians, the Small Catechism also reflects the beliefs of the man who was at the center of a revolution in the history of the church. Like its author, the Small Catechism is ecumenical. It teaches the breadth and depth of the faith held by Christians in a variety of churches around the world. The Small Catechism is also interested in spreading the gospel. Learning his faith from the Bible and in personal experience, Luther came to believe that God created and claimed the whole human race and the planet Earth for the sake of pure love. This trust in God and God's good work with us is at the core of the

*A catechism is a guide for people in need of instruction . . . in the fundamentals of Christian faith.*

Christian faith for the Christians who are called Lutherans.

As the events of the Protestant revolution in 16th-century Europe shook the Western Christian church to its foundations, Luther was quickly convinced of the need for a new catechism. He asked trusted colleagues to take on this project, and they agreed, but then they dawdled with the work. Meanwhile, Luther himself preached several sermons on basic Christian teachings and wrote a number of pamphlets and booklets on the same topics. He quickly turned to the writing of a catechism after returning from official visits to inspect the churches of his German province in the fall of 1528. During the course of this tour he was appalled by the ignorance of both the people and the pastors.

With characteristic energy and fire, he quickly prepared not one but two quite different catechisms simultaneously. The longer of the two, the German Catechism or Large Catechism (1529), was written primarily for pastors and teachers. It is a sort of teacher's guide to the Christian faith. The shorter of the two works became the Small Catechism also published in 1529.

As it came from Luther's hand, the Small Catechism was written to be used in homes and churches by everyone. It was Luther's hope that pastors would make it the foundation of preaching and worship on a regular basis. He also hoped that all Christians would use it as a basis for instruction, discussion, and worship in their own homes. It was with this in mind that Luther arranged to have the Small Catechism printed on posters to be placed in households and churches where all could see and read it. Only later did the Small Catechism appear as a booklet. In time, this cherished work became one of the officially adopted confessions or statements of faith of the Lutheran churches of the world.

As a Lutheran statement of faith, it has been used in a variety of ways. The best known is the preparation of young people for confirmation, sometimes called Affirmation of Baptism in which people make public profession of their faith. It would, however, greatly sadden Luther to think that this association with confirmation has led many to think that the Small Catechism is not for adults but just for young people, or that its primary place is in the schoolrooms of the church. Luther wrote the Small Catechism for all the people of the church and meant it to be used in kitchens by mothers and fathers as much as in classrooms and pulpits by pastors. Luther often said that no one outgrows the need to study the Catechism. In his preface to the Large Catechism Luther wrote of himself, "I do as a child who is being taught the Catechism. Every morning, and whenever else I have time, I read and recite word for word the Lord's Prayer, the Ten Commandments, the Creed, the Psalms, etc. I must still read and study the Catechism daily, yet I cannot master it as I wish, but must remain a child and pupil of the Catechism, and I do it gladly." (*BC* 359.7, 8)

**The parts of the Small Catechism** are very simple in organization and in content. Like the teachers of the ancient church who preceded him, Luther put the Apostles' Creed and the Lord's Prayer at the center of his Catechism. He then added the Ten Commandments at the beginning and material on Baptism and the Lord's Supper at the

*I must still read and study the Catechism daily, yet I cannot master it as I wish but must remain a child and a pupil of the Catechism.*
—Martin Luther

end. He rounded out the whole with some suggestions for prayer and devotion. Finally, he added to the Catechism some instructions about Christian life for various people in different circumstances, the Table of Duties. In many instances, this devotional material and the Table of Duties are not generally printed with the Small Catechism.

The Apostles' Creed, which is at the heart of the Small Catechism, does not come to us directly from the apostles, but it is very ancient. (The word *creed* is from the Latin phrase *credo*, meaning "I believe.") Something like the Apostles' Creed was used very early in the church, perhaps as early as A.D. 200, when new Christians were baptized. Somewhat later it took its present form in the regions we know as Spain and France. After A.D. 800, it was widely used everywhere in the western church. Although not literally from the Scriptures, it reflects the biblical faith in simple but profound words; therefore, it was natural for Luther to put it to use in the Small Catechism. Luther's explanation of the Apostles' Creed, in three simple parts rather than in the cumbersome 12 sections most teachers before him had used, is a brief but powerful summary and explanation of the evangelical faith.

Unlike the Apostles' Creed, the Lord's Prayer is taken directly from the New Testament where it is recorded in two slightly different versions (Matthew 6:9-13 and Luke 11:2-4). The doxology or concluding phrase, "For the kingdom, the power, and the glory are yours, now and forever," does not appear in the New Testament and was not in common use in Luther's day. Therefore, it was not included in his Catechism. But because this doxology has been used by many Christians for centuries, it is often added to the text of the Small Catechism without comment.

Luther put the Ten Commandments at the beginning of his Catechism because he understood the Ten Commandments to contain the demands and promises of the whole Bible. As he said in his preface to the Large Catechism, "Anyone who knows the Ten Commandments perfectly knows the entire Scripture." Like other teachers of the day, Luther slightly changed the text of the Commandments as they appear in Exodus 20:1-17 and Deuteronomy 5:6-21. If you read these passages in the Bible carefully, you will notice that Luther omitted the prohibition of graven images (Exodus 20:4-5) and divided the prohibition of coveting (Exodus 20:17) into two commandments. Luther also added a brief conclusion to the Ten Commandments (from Exodus 20:5-6). These changes explain why Lutherans and Christians of the Reformed traditions sometimes confuse each other when they refer to the Ten Commandments.

When Luther added material on Baptism and the Lord's Supper to his Cate-chism, he did not turn to the theological tradition of the church, but to the New Testament. Large portions of his comments on these two sacraments are direct quotations from the New Testament. They explain in a plain and direct way these events about which Christians have as often said too much as too little.

The Small Catechism also has a section called The Office of the Keys. The name comes from the incident when Jesus said to his follower Peter, "I will give you the keys of the kingdom of heaven, and whatever you bind on earth will be bound in heaven, and whatever you loose on earth will be loosed in heaven" (Matthew 16:19). This was Jesus' direction to the disciples and, therefore, all people of the church to speak his authoritative and effective promise of the forgiveness of sins to one another.

**Using the Small Catechism** can be very helpful in the life of faith. One good way to think of the Small Catechism is to think of it as a guide to the Bible. If you learn the Catechism by heart, for example, you will have committed to memory important parts of the Bible. These verses and Luther's explanations can help you interpret and understand other parts of the Bible that are not as easy to remember or understand. Used this way, the Small Catechism is both a miniature Bible and a guide to reading and studying the whole of the Scriptures.

Bold as it may sound, the Small Catechism can help you map and find your way through your own personal experience. Luther was not exaggerating nor was he being naive or simple-minded when he suggested that the Ten Commandments are a summary of all that we can believe and must do. He intended the Catechism to be a companion in daily life and chose passages from the Bible that are strong and spacious enough to take in all of the complexities of our daily lives.

You certainly will not find in the Small Catechism answers to all of your questions or solutions to all of your problems, but if you keep it in mind and close at hand you will find that it can be an able and faithful guide to the basics of Christian faith, a faith made for real life.

Luther wrote this little book for everyone, young and old alike. Read it. Study it. Mull it over. Poke at it with questions. Talk about it with other Christians. Commit it to memory. Use it in prayer and worship. Make it your own and you will find it a rewarding companion for life.

*The Small Catechism can help you map and find your way through your own personal experience.*

# Ten Words Of Life

**Every day life and death** are at war with each other over planet Earth and the human race. If you find that thought odd, think of what confronts you when you watch the news or read the newspapers. Life and death contend over us endlessly.

Every day we experience the abundance of life in the human community: walls come tumbling down, families endure and thrive, human nobility astounds us, beauty bursts open. Yet, distrust haunts us and death hunts us. Huge armies are poised to march on command; people of the same families and communities perpetrate acts of ghastly violence against each other; twisted imaginations endlessly refine the human capacity for vicious cruelty; ugliness triumphs. Every newscast and every edition of every newspaper reports the latest conflicts of one sort or another between life and death.

Our generation seems especially attuned to this conflict, perhaps because none has known so well as ours that humans are capable of destroying the earth and life itself. The most urgent questions may be these: What will it be for the human race, life or death? What will it be for me, life or death?

Christians entrust and commit themselves to life. They gamble everything they

*Christians entrust and commit themselves to life.*

are and have on the risky notion that people are finally meant not to die, but to live. Christians are not, however, naive or unrealistic about the commitment. They do not think that their faith excuses them from participation in the conflict of life and death. They do not delude themselves into thinking their faith will shield them from the doubts, worries, questions, anxieties, and terrors created by the warfare between life and death. Not in spite of all this, but in the middle of it, Christians confess that God's word of life will have the last word over death; and they stake their lives on that conviction. They do this in the belief that the world has a creator who endowed creation with purpose and meaning, declaring to be on the side of life.

There is no better guide to Christian convictions on the matter of life and death than the Ten Commandments, which are anything but a bundle of crabby "Thou shalt nots." For Christians, who share them with the Jews to whom they were first given, these treasured sentences are ten words of life.

**The First Commandment** is astonishingly personal. It is an introduction spoken directly by an "I" to "you." It leaves no room for a polite look over the shoulder to see if there is somebody else a little easier to talk to in the vicinity.

Without waiting to be asked, the speaker of these words announces himself as "Lord" and "God" and addresses these words to you directly, without an intermediary. The ancient words *Lord* and *God* have been used so often, and sometimes so carelessly, that they can slip easily by us. But listen to them for a moment. The word *Lord* is a title the ancient people of Israel gave to the divine being whom they knew to be God. It is a proper name given to a specific divine being, the creator of heaven and earth, whom the people of Israel confessed to be the living and active God, present among them.

Simply to say that there is such a being, that there is such a God, was then, and is today, a bold statement. Even more surprising is the intention of God to speak directly to you and to lay claim to your attention, your hearing, your capacity to listen to and trust this announcement: "I am the Lord your God."

The First Commandment is God's self-introduction and a declaration of God's intent to claim you for the side of life. In the First Commandment God promises that you are not meant to die, but to live fully, abundantly, richly, fruitfully, creatively, freely. The First Commandment is an oath. It is a promise that God will sustain you in life and that death will not finally have you. It is God's promise to you to take care of you and the human community.

What does this mean for you to whom are these words spoken? Martin Luther was frank in his explanation. You will, first of all, fear this God. You will stand in awe of such a being, for only God has power to create life, to make new, and to create the faith in you that God demands. Because God has

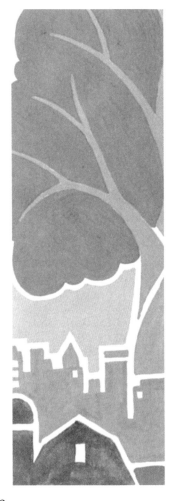

THE FIRST COMMANDMENT

**I am the Lord your God. You shall have no other gods.**

What does this mean for us?

*We are to fear, love, and trust God above anything else.*

13

created and given you all this—life and faith—the First Commandment invites you to respond to God in love. No other "I" will ever lay claim to you in so powerful a way, and no other response but love will finally respond to the graciousness of God.

Finally, the First Commandment means that as a result of God's decision to be God for you, you will want to respond to God by growing in your knowledge of God and God's ways and to trust in God to care for you and for the world. This does not mean that you are invited to exercise yourself in mindless religious fervor. It means that right where you are, in the middle of the conflict between life and death in which we all find ourselves, you have been given the faith necessary to entrust yourself to God for life.

☐ *What does it mean to fear God?*
☐ *How do you feel when you know that someone has accepted you as you are?*
☐ *Bible verses for study:*
*Exod. 20:1-7  Rom. 8:28-39  Eph. 1:3-4*
*Isa. 42:5-9  Psalm 118  John 10:27-30*

### The Second and Third Commandments

are about acoustics—speaking and hearing. The Second Commandment requires that we speak honestly and respectfully of God so that we can hear what God actually says about God's decision for us. When we do that, something else happens: We find ourselves able to speak to God and we discover that God listens to us.

To enter into a conversation like this with God is to pray. Such speaking and listening to God can take place silently or aloud, in the car or in church, in carefully worked out language or in hastily uttered phrases or without conscious words at all. Because the opportunity to listen to God and speak to God in the confidence of being heard is a part of the Christian faith, the language of prayer turns in one way or another to praise and thanksgiving.

THE SECOND COMMANDMENT

**You shall not take the name of the Lord your God in vain.**

What does this mean for us?

*We are to fear and love God so that we do not use his name superstitiously, or use it to curse, swear, lie or deceive, but to call on him in prayer, praise, and thanksgiving.*

14

For the people of Israel, observance of the Third Commandment meant that they were required to set aside the Sabbath day, our Saturday, for rest and reflection. Christians do not understand themselves to be under that obligation, but we observe the day out of the freedom of love and thanksgiving. The Third Commandment continues, however, to remind us of our need to stop and to listen to what God says to us. It invites us to make regular time in our lives to listen, to pray, and to gather for worship. In this way, God makes way for God's promise of life to be heard and to happen.

□ *What does it mean to know God's name?*
□ *If we are able to read the Bible by ourselves, why is so much importance placed on attending worship?*
□ *What are the commands and promises in these two commandments?*
□ *Bible verses for study:*
Exod. 3:1-15    Phil. 2:5-11    Jer. 10:6-10
John 1:1, 14    Isa. 40:6-8    Heb. 1:1-4

THE THIRD COMMANDMENT

**Remember the Sabbath day, to keep it holy.**

What does this mean for us?

*We are to fear and love God so that we do not neglect his Word and the preaching of it, but regard it as holy and gladly hear and learn it.*

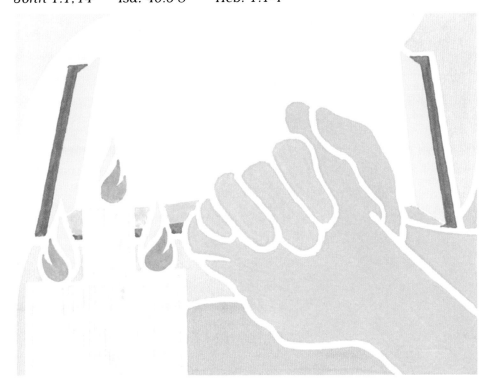

**The Fourth Commandment** teaches us that God has ordered our existence so that we do not live alone but in communities that order and sustain our days. This commandment is focused on the community composed of parents and children but expands its range to include all the patterns of personal contact that make life possible. The family, connections of kinship and friendship, the church, and civil authority are all orders and opportunities given by God for the sake of life. Without these structures, whatever existence we might be able to maintain would be little more than deadly chaos. Relying on them, praying for them, and helping them to be what they were meant to be, our lives can be ordered, peaceful, and fruitful. Asking us to honor and respect those whose task it is to care for and work for us in these spheres, the Fourth Commandment calls on us to enter into the richness of human community willingly and gladly.

☐ *In what ways is being a mother or father an "office"?*
☐ *What is the relationship between the Fourth Commandment and the First Commandment?*
☐ *Bible verses for study:*
*Deut. 6:4-9   Matt. 10:34-37   Psalm 68:5-6*
*Eph. 6:1-4   Rom. 13:1-7   1 Pet. 2:13-17*

THE FOURTH COMMANDMENT
**Honor your father and your mother.**
What does this mean for us?

*We are to fear and love God so that we do not despise or anger our parents and others in authority, but respect, obey, love, and serve them.*

**The Fifth Commandment** is a summons to all people to stand on the side of life. Literally it means, "You shall not murder." It is the forbidding of wanton, lawless violence against life. Certainly, it is not an answer to all the mercilessly difficult questions that go with being human. It does not, for example, forbid military service; nor does it resolve the dilemmas of abortion involving the lives of a child, mother, family, and large communities. The Fifth Commandment does, however, demand that every decision we make be to help preserve and protect life—people and all God's creation. That is why Luther's

THE FIFTH COMMANDMENT
**You shall not kill.**
What does this mean for us?

*We are to fear and love God so that we do not hurt our neighbor in any way, but help him in all his physical needs.*

explanation so clearly orients us toward consideration of our own needs, as well as those of others.

☐ *In what ways can someone kill without lifting a finger against another?*
☐ *How does one decide on matters such as abortion and war?*
☐ *Bible verses for study:*
Gen. 4:1-16    Gen. 9:6-7    1 John 3:14-18
Matt. 5:38-42 Rom. 12:19-21 Psalm 3

**The Sixth Commandment** teaches us that life is the handiwork of a creator who cared deeply about it. As the Bible tells it, the human body is the finest of God's creations, meant to bear physical life into the future. For the sake of companionship and the continuing of creation, men and women are offered the opportunity to enter into marriage, reserving sexual intercourse for their partners in this bond. Others remain single and celibate with God's equal blessing.

This commandment helps people see, as a fundamental condition of life itself, that human beings care for their own bodies and respect those of others. Observed with love, the Sixth Commandment is a blessing on both present and future generations.

☐ *Why do people feel guilty about their own bodies? What does this guilt cause a person to do?*
☐ *What does friendship have to do with this commandment?*
☐ *Bible verses for study:*
Psalm 128      Gen. 2:18-25  1 Cor. 6:15-20
Mark 10:6-12

**The Seventh Commandment** has a simple message. Before things are mine or yours to use, they are God's to own. And God directs our use of possessions for the benefit of others. This commandment has a sharply honed negative edge. We are not to take from others, either through outright steal-

THE SIXTH COMMANDMENT
**You shall not commit adultery.**
What does this mean for us?

*We are to fear and love God so that in matters of sex our words and conduct are pure and honorable, and husband and wife love and respect each other.*

THE SEVENTH COMMANDMENT
**You shall not steal.**
What does this mean for us?

*We are to fear and love God so that we do not take our neighbor's money or property, or get them in any dishonest way, but help him to improve and protect his property and means of making a living.*

ing or in legal but still wrong ways. This applies to us both as individuals and as members of contending human communities. This commandment has a surprisingly positive edge as well. We are to regard our possessions as means to an end—the good of our neighbors. The secret is knowing the difference between ownership and use. All things belong to God. They are given to us both to enjoy for ourselves and to use for the good of others.

☐ *Why is there such an emphasis on property and material goods in our society?*
☐ *How can certain advertisements be stealing?*
☐ *Bible verses for study:*
*1 Pet. 4:9-11   Matt. 25:14-30  Lev. 19:35-36*
*Matt. 5:38-42  Gal. 5:13-15*

**The Eighth Commandment** is about how to get along with other people. You can utterly destroy other people by peddling lies about them. In this commandment, God makes possible another way. Life can be all that it was meant to be only when we speak the truth to one another and about one another. Truthful communication is essential to human existence. Even more, creative and constructive talk is necessary for abundant lives. Words, the Eighth Commandment indicates, are better used for defense than for attack, for kindness rather than cruelty, for encouragement rather than judgment.

☐ *Why is it easier to repeat bad things about others than good things?*
☐ *Why is it difficult to confront someone who has wronged you?*
☐ *Bible verses for study:*
*Matt. 18:15-17  Zech. 8:14-17  Prov. 31:8-9*
*John 10:1-5      1 Pet. 4:7-8     Luke 6:37-38*

THE EIGHTH COMMANDMENT

**You shall not bear false witness against your neighbor.**

What does this mean for us?

*We are to fear and love God so that we do not betray, slander, or lie about our neighbor, but defend him, speak well of him, and explain his actions in the kindest way.*

**The Ninth and the Tenth Commandments**
are in one sense a commentary on the Seventh and the Eighth Commandments.
These two final words of life reach farther than our behavior. They ask us not only to govern our actions, but also to examine our consciences. They invite us to reorient our inclinations away from ourselves and toward others. To ponder these commandments is finally to examine our whole life in the light of the Ten Commandments.

☐ *How do these two commandments relate to the other eight?*
☐ *How do we become slaves to things?*
☐ *How does God use these commandments to protect us from ourselves?*
☐ *Bible verses for study:*
*Rom. 15:4-6    1 Kings 21:1-16 Amos 5:11-24*
*Luke 12:15-21 James 1:12-18  Col. 3:1-5*

**What does God say of all these commandments?** There is a slack and false version of the Christian faith holding that God's promises to forgive our shortcomings means that we are relieved from the consequences of our behavior or exempt from punishment when we violate the Ten Commandments. This final word added to the Ten Commandments tells the truth. Our behavior does have unavoidable consequences. What we do with our loyalties, our

**You shall not covet your neighbor's house.**

What does this mean for us?

*We are to fear and love God so that we do not desire to get our neighbor's possessions by scheming, or by pretending to have a right to them, but always help him keep what is his.*

THE TENTH COMMANDMENT

**You shall not covet your neighbor's wife, or his manservant, or his maidservant, or his cattle, or anything that is your neighbor's.**

What does this mean for us?

*We are to fear and love God so that we do not tempt or coax away from our neighbor his wife or his workers, but encourage them to remain loyal.*

WHAT DOES GOD SAY OF ALL THESE COMMANDMENTS?

**He says: "I, the Lord your God, am a jealous God, visiting the iniquity of the fathers upon the children to the third generation and fourth generation of those who hate me, but showing steadfast love to**

19

actions, and our bodies matters deeply to God. The Ten Commandments are a summons to commit ourselves and our behaviors to the cause of life. They are a call to a rigorous and strenuous vitality. They warn us that to stray from their ways is to fall into destructive error.

More than that, however, the Ten Commandments are ten words that offer us life rich beyond imagining. They tell us of a God who speaks directly to us and who makes an unbreakable promise to care for us. They protect our ability to hear and speak to God. They locate us in the human community and show us how to trust and love one another in the same way that God trusts and loves each one of us. Anything but a fistful of harsh "Thou shalt nots," the commandments are ten words of life.

□ *How can the cycle of God's wrath be broken when God says he will visit the "iniquity of the fathers upon the children"? What hope can we have?*
□ *What room is there for a word of grace?*
□ *Bible verses for study:*
*Gen. 8:20-22    Ezek. 18:1-24    Rom. 8:1-11*
*Psalm 14          1 John 5:1-5      Gal. 3:10-14*

**thousands of those who love me and keep my commandments."**

What does this mean for us?

*God warns that he will punish all who break these commandments. Therefore we are to fear his wrath and not disobey him. But he promises grace and every blessing to all who keep these commandments. Therefore we are to love and trust them and gladly do what he commands.*

---

**1.** It has often been said that the First Commandment summarizes all that we need to know about God. In what ways does that seem right to you?

**2.** The first three commandments speak of God's relationship to you and your relationship to God. How does your understanding of these commandments shape the way you think about the remaining seven?

# For Reflection

**3.** Seven of the Ten Commandments are stated in negative form ("You shall not . . ."). Rewrite one of the seven in positive form and see what happens. Which form best expresses the idea that the commandments are ten words of life?

**4.** Reflect on the Ten Commandments as promises from God. They are markers over the aspects of life God considers most important and at the same time are most vulnerable to human evil. In light of this reflection, what can you say about God's will for the human community?

**5.** Use the Ten Commandments as a mirror in which to examine your own life. What do you discover about yourself and God's will for you and the people whose lives touch your own?

Identify the commandment that is most uplifting and encouraging to you and the commandment that most troubles and oppresses you. Take a few minutes to reflect on your life in light of both.

You may want to close your meditation with the following or another prayer.

We come to you, Lord, as our God. We come in fear, in love, and in trust. We ask you to forgive us for our shortcomings and to help us enter more fully into the abundant lives you intend us and all people to enjoy. Amen.

You may want to read aloud and commit to memory the following Bible verse.

"I shall not die, but I shall live, and recount the deeds of the Lord" (Psalm 118:17).

## Our Prayers

# God Three Times Over

**Not long ago** a team of sociologists studied life in the United States and wrote a book called *Habits of the Heart*. In it, the authors described several kinds or types of contemporary Americans. One of these recognizable types of people, with the fictional name of Sheila Larson, described her religious faith this way: "I believe in God. . . . My faith has carried me a long way. It's Sheila-ism. Just my own little voice" (page 121). Her "voice," Sheila said, told her to be good to herself and kind to others. That is the sum of her faith. You may recognize it.

Christians think and believe that there is more than this to authentic faith in God. While they honor the testimony of personal experience and conscience, Christians also tune their lives to the sound of another voice. Christians trust that God speaks to them from beyond the limits of their own experience. To hear the voice of God they turn to the pages of the Bible and they gather regularly with other Christians to read from the Bible and to listen to what it says. But the Bible is a sprawling collection of 66 books written over the course of thousands of years and is not always easy to comprehend or remember.

The people of the church recognized this problem centuries ago and over time

*Christians trust that God speaks to them from beyond the limits of their own experience.*

assembled several short statements of faith intended to summarize the message of Scripture. One of the best known and most widely used of these statements is the Apostles' Creed. Although not written by the apostles, it is intended to be a compact, memorable summary of the essentials of Christian faith.

As such, the Apostles' Creed has served for centuries to direct the attention of the church to a voice not its own, the voice of the living God. Not because it was old or widely used, but because it is a trustworthy guide to the teaching of Scripture, Martin Luther chose to put the Apostles' Creed at the center of the Small Catechism.

Simple in expression and easy to remember, the Apostles' Creed is often divided into three sections, or articles, for study and reflection. This threefold division grows naturally out of the Christian conviction that while there is only one God. This God's self-revelation to us is as Father, as Son, and as Holy Spirit. For this reason, Luther divided the Apostles' Creed into three articles, or parts, corresponding to the work of the Trinity, or the three "persons" who are the one God.

**The First Article of the Apostles' Creed** concerns humanity's relationship to God, life, and the world; but Luther's answer to these questions is not what most people at first expect.

Questions about the origin of the universe and the planet Earth have fascinated people for centuries. This has been especially true during recent times when enormous strides in the study of the natural sciences have given us dazzling new insights into the history of the universe and the human race. Christians and others debate both the facts and their meaning intensely. Did God really fashion the world in six days and rest on the seventh? What about the Big Bang? Did God make human beings in the way Genesis 2 teaches or in the way Genesis 1

THE FIRST ARTICLE

**I believe in God, the Father Almighty, creator of heaven and earth.**

What does this mean?

*I believe that God has created me and all that exists. He has given me and still preserves my body and soul with all their powers.*

*He provides me with food and clothing, home and family, daily work, and all I need from day to day. God also protects me in every danger and guards me from every evil.*

*All this he does out of fatherly and divine goodness and mercy, though I do not deserve it. Therefore, I surely ought to thank and praise, serve and obey him.*

*This is most certainly true.*

24

teaches? Did the human race evolve through a complex process of natural selection? Do different answers to these immensely important questions complement or conflict with one another?

Significant as these questions are, the Small Catechism would have us consider the capacity to answer these questions less important than the ability to trust ourselves to certain truths—truths even larger than those illuminated by any of these questions or the competing answers to them.

In his explanation of the First Article, Luther insisted that we understand it personally. The "I" and the "me" of Luther's explanation are you. The message is this: Whatever the facts of ancient history or contemporary physics, your life is not of your own making. You did not bring yourself to birth, nor can you take the least credit for the origin of any of the things that sustain your life. What you eat, what you wear, the shelter you call home, the people you think of as family, the work you do, all the things essential to life are sheer and unearned gifts.

The maker and giver of these gifts is God. Following the Bible, the Creed invites us to remember that God does not simply create and abandon the world as if it were a self-winding clock or self-sustaining organism. God is always at the work of creating and sustaining the world, caring for it "from day to day" as the Small Catechism puts it.

Readers of the Small Catechism may have at least two troubling questions about Luther's explanation of the First Article. First, what about those who do not have sufficient food and clothing, home and family, work and all that they need? Beneath Luther's celebration of God's creative work is the acknowledgement of human responsibility for the creation and the opportunity to join with God in the care of it. When some are deprived, not all acknowledge that God intends these gifts to be given to all.

Second, if God really protects us from danger and evil, how can our lives be as troubled and difficult as they often are? Martin Luther was anything but naive about the facts of life. The faith Luther taught in the Small Catechism is remarkable for its realism. Luther knew that Christian faith would not protect us from physical danger, illness, questions without answers, the experience of doubt, moments of deep personal agony, or the experience of death. Luther's point was that in and through all of this God contends for life, and that at the end of time God will raise us from the dead and renew our lives yet again. As we will see later in the explanation of the Creed, God will make and sustain new life even from the death that will inevitably come to each of us.

It is not accidental that Luther reversed the order of the Creed in his explanation. He spoke at length of God as creator before he explicitly spoke of God as Father. This is consistent with the purpose of the First Article of the Creed, which, as Luther said elsewhere, is meant not only to show us the work and the will, but the nature of God as well.

If God had only made the world and let it be, it might have been sufficient to call God "creator." But in God's making and sustaining of the world and its creatures, God reveals a passionate love for creation. But God as creator is not the only way of God's revelation to us. God's self-revelation has been described as that of a good and loving Father.

God is not Father because of creation, as though God were the progenetor. The title *Father* arises out of God's merciful redeeming, saving us and all of creation. God is Father by adopting us through God's own act of redeeming us—as God redeemed Israel from Egypt and as God redeemed us through Jesus Christ. Our relationship with God does not begin with our rights established by creation. God begins with us

26

in a relationship established by God's sheer unqualified self-giving. It is in this way that we can understand the biblical term *Father* apart from the sometimes sorry history of human fathers and their children.

☐ *If God created the world and called it good, how do you account for killing storms, diseases, and natural disasters?*
☐ *What is meant by the statement "created in God's image" (Genesis 1:27)?*
☐ *How can you tell if someone is going to keep a promise made to you? What does it mean to trust?*
☐ *Bible verses for study:*
Psalm 8        Matt. 6:25-33    Job 38–41
Gen. 1:1—2:4a   Rom. 4:13-25   Psalm 139

**The Second Article of the Apostles' Creed**
is at the center of the Christian faith. Christians believe that Jesus of Nazareth, who lived nearly 2000 years ago, was the son of a young woman named Mary and of God, the creator of all that lives. Christians confess that Jesus used a short public ministry to preach, teach, and do astonishing things in the name of God. When the world would tolerate him no longer, he was crucified under the supervision of a minor official of the Roman Empire, Pontius Pilate. Three days after his death, God raised Jesus from the dead to assure all people of the final victory of life over death. By the death of Christ on the cross, God redeemed all humanity. In Christ's death, God makes us righteous. At the end of time all those whom God has saved will be raised from the dead. On that day, Jesus will return to sit as judge over all people. This is the history recited by the Apostles' Creed in short, terse sentences.

As in his comments on the First Article, Luther gave the story an intensely personal note. The "I" and the "my" again refer to you. To confess that God creates the faith you need means not only that you are able to affirm the power of God in the world, but

HELL BEING ABSENT FROM GOD

**I believe in Jesus Christ, his only Son, our Lord. He was conceived by the power of the Holy Spirit, and born of the virgin Mary. He suffered under Pontius Pilate, was crucified, died, and was buried. He descended into hell. On the third day he rose again. He ascended into heaven, and is seated at the right hand of the Father. He will come again to judge the living and the dead.**

What does this mean?

*I believe that Jesus Christ—true God, Son of the Father from eternity, and true man, born of the Virgin Mary—is my Lord.*

*At great cost he has saved and redeemed me, a lost and condemned person. He has freed me from sin, death, and the power of the devil—not with silver or gold, but with his holy and precious blood and his innocent suffering and death.*

*All this he has done that I may be his own, live under him in his kingdom and serve him in everlasting righteousness, innocence, and blessedness, just as he is risen from the dead and lives and rules eternally.*

*This is most certainly true.*

that you can recognize and trust Jesus of Nazareth as the one person who cares for and governs your life. To acknowledge this gift of faith is to know that your life is not in your own hands, but in God's.

But why did God send Jesus to die? Could God not simply have named him Lord? The answer of Scripture, in the Creed, and expanded by Luther in the Small Catechism, is this: Jesus died to destroy sin and death.

The Christian faith is, in this respect, brutally realistic. It knows that humans are capable of great evil and that their lives are deeply troubled and affected by that capacity. Christians believe that human beings are sinful and that they act sinfully. Further, Christians believe that evil in the world is not merely disorganized trouble, but that it is a formidable, coherent force personified in what the Bible calls the devil. The result of all sin and evil is death—death for individuals and death for the human race and the planet itself.

God is the sworn enemy of evil, of sin, death, and the devil. Jesus Christ is the way God put an end to sin and evil. The resurrection of Jesus from the dead is the first proof of God's ultimate victory over death. God used Jesus' death to destroy death and to make life—now and in the future—possible for us. Although the Bible speaks of this in many ways, Luther used the particular biblical picture of a ransom to explain God's work in Jesus on our behalf. Humans are hostages to evil who have been set free by God. God has graciously secured our freedom from death, not with the payment of money, but by the sacrifice of a deeply loved son on our behalf.

God has done this so that we may live as we were created by God to live—as creatures in a world fashioned for our good. The resurrection of Jesus from the dead is a signal from the future that as it once was, so it will be once again. The old life of sin and death are destroyed and replaced by the new life of faith and life. The promise of resurrection is given to all who believe.

In the meantime, we can live day by day confident of that future. We can be deeply engaged in the life of the world that was created and loved by God and saved through the death and resurrection of Jesus Christ.

☐ What do you think about and how do you act when you know that someone has sacrificed something for your sake?
☐ Jesus suffered, died, and was raised again. What does that say to you when you are suffering?
☐ Why do you think God chose to become human in Jesus?
☐ Bible verses for study:
Isa. 53        Luke 2:1-20     Eph. 1:20-23
Mark 8:27-33   Gal. 2:19-21    Rom. 3:21-31

**The Third Article of the Apostles' Creed** brings together what it means to have faith in God as revealed in Jesus Christ.

If all of what the Creed and Luther have said is true, but not true for you, it will make little difference in your life. That is why God does not leave it up to you. Left to yourself with the knowledge of God as creator and the story of Jesus you would not be able to believe it or entrust yourself to it.

It is the work of the Holy Spirit of God to bring you to trust this story as your own and to join you to a community of others who know the same trust. With the Scriptures in hand, Luther insisted that no exercise of your mind or effort of your will, however strenuous, can bring you to faith. To a people like us, accustomed to deciding every important question for ourselves, this is utterly shocking. But neither Bible nor Catechism will relent here. It is the work of God to bring us to faith, and the Holy Spirit is God's invincible power at work for our good.

God is irrevocably committed to gathering believers to himself. To see to that end, God intervenes in our lives without asking

THE THIRD ARTICLE

**I believe in the Holy Spirit, the holy catholic church, the communion of saints, the forgiveness of sins, the resurrection of the body, and life everlasting. Amen.**

What does this mean?

*I believe that I cannot by my own understanding or effort believe in Jesus Christ my Lord, or come to him. But the Holy Spirit has called me through the Gospel, enlightened me with his gifts, and sanctified and kept me in true faith.*

*In the same way he calls, gathers, enlightens, and sanctifies the whole Christian church on earth, and keeps it united with Jesus Christ in the one true faith.*

*In this Christian church day after day he fully forgives my sins and the sins of all believers. On the last day he will raise me and all the dead and give me and all believers in Christ eternal life.*

*This is most certainly true.*

our permission. God chooses us and adopts us as children without relying on us to ask for it to be done. All of this saving comes through the faith that God gives.

Faith is a word for the most personal and intimate of relationships. To enter into faith is akin to falling in love. To live in faith is to entrust yourself to God's judgment on your life and to accept God's love for you; it is to be caught up by God's causes in the world; it is to abandon yourself to a rigorous and risky way of life so taxing that even mature and life-long Christians falter when they think of it. Faith can only be experienced to be truly understood.

At the same time, faith rests on nothing of our own doing. Finally, faith is a work of God in us, reflecting the reality that we do not choose God, but that God chooses us for life, for good, forever. "Give me a lover," the Christian leader and theologian named Augustine (A.D. 354–430) once said, "and that person will know what I am talking about."

There is no other aspect of Christian faith and life so difficult to understand as the conviction that God does not ask us to decide for him before making it known that God has decided for us. To learn that we are not in charge of our lives is a troubling thought; but in the end to know this is a source of great comfort and strength. It is to understand that God is earnestly for us and that we are not meant to die, but to live.

There is always this troubling question: How do you know if you are among the chosen? You are hearing this story, so you can be sure that it is for you. But what about others? They can hear this story, also, if you or someone else will tell it to them. The Scriptures teach that God wishes all people to live and flourish.

It is a source of great encouragement to Christians to remember that they do not live the life of faith alone. God gives an abundance of gifts of different kinds in dif-

ferent measures to us as members of a community called the church. It is only in this community that all of these gifts add up to a way of life.

There are no Christian soloists. It is only through the life of the church that God calls people to faith. This is where God gathers them to live together, where they are given gifts for service, and where they practice the life of faith. It is only through the life of the church that this story is made known and believed, that the forgiveness of sins and the promise of life as it was meant to be lived are made known.

The statement of faith called the Apostles' Creed ends where it begins—with the gift of abundant life. As creator, God gave us life as a sheer gift. As redeemer, Jesus Christ took our lives from the clutches of a deathly evil that had possessed us. As Spirit, God ushers us into a community of faith where life is lived to the fullest (even in the midst of suffering and death) and where the promise of an endless new life after death is always before us.

□ What is the role of the Holy Spirit in God "three times over"?

□ What does it mean that God chooses us and adopts us as children without relying on us to ask for it to be done?

□ What does it mean for you to be called by God to be part of "the holy catholic church"?

□ Bible verses for study:

| | | |
|---|---|---|
| Ps. 139:7-12 | Joel 2:28-32 | John 20:19-23 |
| Acts 2 | John 3:1-17 | Gal. 5:16-26 |

*It is a source of great encouragement to Christians to remember that they do not live the life of faith alone.*

**1.** Describe the nature and work of the three persons of the Trinity as they are described in the Apostles' Creed.

**2.** How would you interpret Luther's explanation of the First Article of the Apostles' Creed to someone without a home or enough to eat?

**3.** In his explanation of the Second Article, Luther used the idea of a ransom to explain the effect of Jesus' death. What other concepts could you use or do you recall from the New Testament? See John 3:14-17; Romans 3:21-26; Galatians 3:13-15; 4:4-5; and Hebrews 7:24-28.

**4.** How does the notion that we cannot believe in Jesus Christ or come to him through our own understanding or effort fit together with an understanding of faith as trust?

**Our Prayers**

When you are alone, recite the phrases of the Apostles' Creed slowly aloud. Pause after each phrase and allow yourself to enter into its message. Take a few moments to reflect on the meaning of what you have learned for your life. If you are with a group, each member might speak briefly about what she or he has come to learn from study of the Apostles' Creed and Luther's Small Catechism. Alone or in a group, let any new insights prompt moments of prayer in conclusion.

*Conversation w God*

# How To Pray

***Prayer***—the mention of the word may put you off. Perhaps you have never really prayed. Or it may be that when you think of prayer, you recall prayers mumbled at bedtime in childhood or of tiresome exercises in religion endured or abandoned as an adult. Prayer for you may be words whispered to the sky in a pinch. On the other hand, prayer may be a rewarding part of your life practiced for many years. In any case, the Lord's Prayer has something to offer you. It is safe enough to wade in and deep enough to swim in at the same time.

Matthew and Luke's gospels tell that the followers of Jesus asked him how to pray. In answer, Jesus taught them to pray and himself offered a prayer we call the Lord's Prayer or the Our Father from its first words.

Jesus told his disciples that there was more to prayer than mere words. He taught them not only what to pray, but how to pray. The Lord's Prayer is meant to teach us a way of praying as well as words to use. It is not at all surprising that Matthew and Luke recall the Lord's Prayer in somewhat different words. Knowing this may help us better enter into the riches of the Lord's Prayer and the depth of Luther's interpretation of it.

Before turning to the Lord's Prayer, we might stop to ask what it means to pray and why we ought to pray at all. The Bible and the Small Catechism answer both questions clearly.

What is prayer? To pray is to speak with God the way one would talk to a good parent. God, like any father or mother worthy of the name, wants to talk with his children and to respond as is best for them.

Why pray? At the end of Luther's explanation of the Lord's Prayer, there is a definite answer to this question. It is, of course, a good and natural thing for children to talk to their parents, but there is more to it than that. Christians consider themselves to be a people under orders from God. They pray, in the first place, because God commanded them to do so and because God promised to hear and answer their prayers. Because prayer is for many Christians a strenuous and taxing discipline, it is well to know and rely on both command and promise. If you are one of the many for whom prayer is unknown or difficult and forbidding rather than easy and pleasurable, take comfort. God has asked you to do this and promises to hear you when you pray. Furthermore, the apostle Paul said that the Holy Spirit prays for us when we are unable (Romans 8:26).

**The Introduction and the First, Second, and Third Petitions** of the Lord's Prayer set the stage for the whole prayer. The first words of the Lord's Prayer, "Our Father," are intended to remind us that God welcomes us and covets conversation with us. They are a promise to us that God cares deeply about us as parents care for their children. These simple words are an invitation to speak with confidence with someone who can always be counted on to be for us. At the same time, they are a reminder of our own identity. We are the children of this God.

THE INTRODUCTION

**Our Father in heaven.**

What does this mean?

*Here God encourages us to believe that he is truly our Father and we are his children. We therefore are to pray to him with complete confidence just as children speak to their loving father.*

THE FIRST PETITION

**Hallowed be your name.**

What does this mean?

*God's name certainly is holy in itself, but we ask in this prayer that we may keep it holy.*

When does this happen?

*God's name is hallowed whenever his Word is taught in its truth and purity and we as children of God live in harmony with it. Help us to do this, heavenly Father!*

*But anyone who teaches or lives contrary to the Word of God dishonors God's name among us. Keep us from doing this, heavenly Father!*

These three petitions are huge in design. Someone has remarked that they keep our prayers from being too small. They are not so much about God's name, message, rule, or even God's will, as they are about us. As Luther pointed out, God can take care of name, kingdom, and will for himself and does. In different ways, these petitions all ask God to use us to tell the good news and to tell it the way God meant it to be told. They ask that our lives reflect God's ways and God's rule over the world.

The way Luther spoke of these prayers is revealing. He was certain—as you can be when you pray them—that God will answer them. He did not ask if God will answer these requests, but simply asked when.

Be aware that if in faith you make these prayers your own, God will answer them. You may, however, be staggered by the answers because the emphasis is always on God's initiative and God's intention to make you a part of the answer to these prayers: "Hallowed be *your* name. *Your* kingdom come. *Your* will be done." God uses our prayers and God's response to them to accomplish his work in the world. An old rabbi once put it this way: "God's abundance fills the world at all times. . . . If our words of prayer . . . are concentrated upon God, they unite with his abundance and form the channel through which it descends upon the world."

☐ *What does it mean to pray with complete confidence?*
☐ *What do we gain when we pray the first two petitions?*
☐ *Why should we pray for ourselves?*
☐ *Why do we pray "Your will be done" when we know the "will of God is surely done without our prayer"?*
☐ *Bible verses for study:*
*Eph. 3:20-21   1 Thess. 5:16-18  Acts 4:23-31*
*1 Sam. 2:1-10  Matt. 6:5-15*

THE SECOND PETITION

**Your kingdom come.**

What does this mean?

*God's kingdom comes indeed without our praying for it, but we ask in this prayer that it may come also to us.*

When does this happen?

*God's kingdom comes when our heavenly Father gives us his Holy Spirit, so that by his grace we believe his holy Word and live a godly life on earth now and in heaven forever.*

THE THIRD PETITION

**Your will be done, on earth as in heaven.**

What does this mean?

*The good and gracious will of God is surely done without our prayer, but we ask in this prayer that it may be done also among us.*

When does this happen?

*God's will is done when he hinders and defeats every evil scheme and purpose of the devil, the world, and our sinful self, which would prevent us from keeping his name holy and would oppose the coming of his kingdom. And his will is done when he strengthens our faith and keeps us firm in his Word as long as we live. This is his gracious and good will.*

**The Fourth Petition,** much like the First Petition, is not so much a request that God will give us our daily bread—representing all that we need to live—but that God will make us aware that these things are gifts to us from a creator ceaselessly at work for our good and the good of all people. In the explanation to the First Article of the Apostles' Creed, Luther wrote that if some people do not have what they need to live, it may be because all people do not recognize that things are given to us by a God upon whom everyone depends for life.

☐ *Why does the petition ask for "daily bread" instead of asking for future gifts?*
☐ *What does it mean that all things come from God?*
☐ *Bible verses for study:*
*Matt. 4:1-11     Exod. 16:1-21     Psalm 90*

THE FOURTH PETITION

**Give us today our daily bread.**

What does this mean?

*God gives daily bread, even without our prayer, to all people, though sinful, but we ask in this prayer that he will help us to realize this and to receive our daily bread with thanks.*

What is meant by "daily bread"?

*Daily bread includes everything needed for this life, such as food and clothing, home and property, work and income, a devoted family, an orderly community, good government, favorable weather, peace and health, a good name, and true friends and neighbors.*

**The Fifth Petition** asks for the most important of the gifts of life, the forgiveness of our sins. Through this petition we are aware that the most ardent Christians battle against their own sin all their lives. No one can leave this behind and enter each new day without the forgiveness only God can grant. As Luther stated in the Sacrament of Holy Communion in the Small Catechism, "where there is forgiveness of sins, there is also life and salvation." This prayer asks not only for forgiveness for you, but also asks for the power, courage, will, and ability for you to forgive those who have wronged you.

There is, however, a trap here that can take away all the joy of the forgiven life. This petition does not mean that God will forgive your sins only if you forgive others. It means rather that God's forgiveness makes possible and is represented in your forgiveness of others.

☐ *Why is it so difficult to forgive someone?*
☐ *Why is it difficult to believe the words, "You are forgiven for Jesus' sake"?*
☐ *Bible verses for study:*
*1 Pet. 1:3-9      1 Pet. 5:6-11      Rom. 6:1-11*

**The Sixth Petition** is not a request for protection against bad decisions or wrong behavior. Important as those things are, this prayer is about something still more important. It asks God to keep us by grace in a relation of trust and confidence. It is a request that God keep us in the gift of faith so that we can continue to receive all of its benefits—forgiveness and life.

☐ *Why do we want something all the more when we are told we cannot have it?*
☐ *How does it feel to know you have broken trust with someone you love?*
☐ *Bible verses for study:*
*Psalm 30     2 Tim. 4:17-18     2 Thess. 3:1-5*

THE FIFTH PETITION

**Forgive us our sins as we forgive those who sin against us.**

What does this mean?

*We ask in this prayer that our Father in heaven would not hold our sins against us and because of them refuse to hear our prayer. And we pray that he would give us everything by grace, for we sin every day and deserve nothing but punishment. So we on our part will heartily forgive and gladly do good to those who sin against us.*

THE SIXTH PETITION

**Save us from the time of trial.**

What does this mean?

*God tempts no one to sin, but we ask in this prayer that God would watch over us and keep us so that the devil, the world, and our sinful self may not deceive us and draw us into false belief, despair, and other great and shameful sins. And we pray that even though we are so tempted we may still win the final victory.*

**The Seventh Petition** ends the Lord's Prayer where our own prayers often begin— with the request that God protect us from danger. It also asks God to tend us when we enter into an experience no human evades, death. That this petition comes last rather than first is a study in our priorities and the nature of God's goodness to us.

☐ God gives us his word in times of trouble. What good is that?
☐ Why is it best to end the Lord's Prayer with this petition rather than to begin the prayer with it?
☐ Bible verses for study:
Isa. 43:1-3   Rom. 8:18-25   1 Cor. 13:9-13

THE SEVENTH PETITION

**And deliver us from evil.**

What does this mean?

*We ask in this inclusive prayer that our heavenly Father would save us from every evil to body and soul, and at our last hour would mercifully take us from the troubles of this world to himself in heaven.*

**The Doxology** of the Lord's Prayer, traditionally added by many Christians today, are words of confidence. They are a way of saying that we know God can and will answer the prayers Jesus taught us to make. To say "Amen" is no more than to say all of that at once. If someone else is leading in prayer and you add your Amen, it is a way of making the prayer your own.

☐ How does the Doxology summarize the whole prayer?
☐ Amen means "I agree." With which of the petitions do you have the most difficulty agreeing?
☐ Bible verses for study:
Psalm 23   Luke 2:25-38   Rev. 22:12-21

THE DOXOLOGY

**For the kingdom, the power, and the glory are yours, now and forever. Amen.**

What does "Amen" mean?

*Amen means Yes, it shall be so. We say Amen because we are certain that such petitions are pleasing to our Father in heaven and are heard by him. For he himself has commanded us to pray in this way and has promised to hear us.*

**1.** Prayer is often defined as "conversation with God." Can you identify other ways of talking that you might also use as prayer?

**2.** Luther used the present tense when he speaks of the rule of God over our lives: "God's kingdom comes. . . ." What does the Lord's Prayer reveal about life in the kingdom of God?

**3.** How would you speak of the Lord's Prayer to people alienated from their parents or without them? To someone starving?

**4.** What does the order of petitions in the Lord's Prayer have to say to the ordering of priorities in our lives, and what does it teach about God's way with us?

# For Reflection

Regardless of the language in which it is prayed, the Lord's Prayer binds all Christians throughout the world in Christ. But recall that the Lord's Prayer is not a prayer to recite by memory as a religious exercise. It opens us to the things for which Christ would have us pray, and it also teaches us how to pray.

According to Matthew and Luke, Jesus taught this prayer at the request of his disciples. Luke recorded the following situation in which Jesus taught this prayer: "He [Jesus] was praying in a certain place, and after he had finished, one of his disciples said to him, 'Lord, teach us to pray, as John taught his disciples' " (Luke 11:1). And Jesus taught them.

Pray the Lord's Prayer slowly, petition by petition, allowing time to reflect on what Jesus was teaching in each petition. If you wish, make your reflection aloud in the form of a prayer to God.

# Our Prayers

Our Father in heaven,
 hallowed be your name,
 your kingdom come,
 your will be done,
 on earth as in heaven.
Give us today our daily
 bread.
Forgive us our sins
 as we forgive those
 who sin against us.
Save us from the time of
 trial
 and deliver us from evil.
For the kingdom, the
 power,
 and the glory are yours
 now and forever. Amen.

# From Death To **Life**

**The Bible teaches** that God's most important means of communicating with us is the announcement of the gospel, the message of Jesus' life, death, and resurrection. Ordinary spoken words in the service of this gospel are the instruments God uses to create the faith in us that God demands. With this gift of faith, we are saved. To receive all that God intends you to have—forgiveness of sin, life, and salvation—it is enough for you to hear this message and trust God's Word.

In order to encourage and strengthen our confidence that the message of Jesus' life and death and resurrection is true and that it can deliver what it promises, Jesus twice connected physical signs to his spoken words. He connected water to his promise of life and, right before he died, he took the simple elements of bread and wine and bound them to the promise of the forgiveness of our sins.

The church gave the name *sacrament* to both of the promises to which Jesus attached physical signs—water, bread, and wine. These sacraments are called Baptism and the Lord's Supper. They are God's promises to us. The sacraments are "visible words" for us to see and feel as well as to hear. Finally, however, they can only be be-

*Ordinary spoken words in the service of this gospel are the instruments God uses to work his way in us.*

lieved and trusted. And even this faith or trust to believe God's word in the sacraments is a gift of God. Even if we despise God's word and the sacraments, they remain true and valid. Luther wrote in the Large Catechism that if some despiser of Baptism desired to be baptized, we should baptize "in all good faith." The Baptism would be valid. "For there would be water together with God's word, even though he failed to receive it properly" (*BC* 443.54).

God's word given in Baptism is not just a word as one person would speak to another. It is the original word that at once tears down and creates anew. God's word is "like a hammer that breaks a rock in pieces" (Jeremiah 23:29). It is the word that brought into being all of creation (Genesis 1).

Through Baptism we are not simply repaired or refurbished as one would fix up an old house. It is not a mere washing away of the dirt of our lives that leaves our old selves cleaner but still intact. God's word in Baptism literally kills the old sinful self in us. As Paul wrote, "Do you not know that all of us who have been baptized in Christ Jesus were baptized into his death?" (Romans 6:3). Yet, God does not leave us in death but raises us up into a completely new life in Christ. Again, as Paul wrote, "As Christ was raised from the dead by the glory of the Father, so we too might walk in newness of life" (Romans 6:4b).

So that we do not miss God's word of death to new life, Christ attached his word to ordinary water that we can see and feel as it washes over us.

We can sometimes miss a human word spoken to us, but we cannot easily miss getting wet. It is as if Christ says to each of us by name, "Here in this water you know my decision to save you. Now you can be certain, for I have washed you with my sure word of promise."

*God's word in Baptism literally kills the old sinful self in us.*

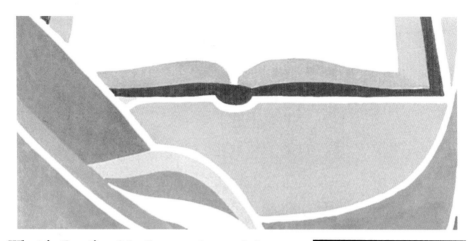

**What is Baptism?** Luther emphasized that Baptism depends on the promise of God. More than that, Luther reminds us, Jesus has ordered those who follow him in faith to practice Baptism, washing new Christian believers with water in the name of God the Father, the Son, and the Holy Spirit. It is good to know that and to rely on it. We are, in this case, not left to our own devices. We are acting under orders.

At the same time, Baptism is not "magic." It is not merely a physical act to be performed or endured. The water of Baptism is not like the crystals in which some people put their confidence, or a rabbit's foot carried for luck, or a talisman worn for security. As insurance against life's disasters, it is useless. The water is simply water, essential to life, but still only water. It is the promise of God that is the active ingredient in this recipe. It is the Word of God used together with water that makes Baptism an event that creates new life in us.

☐ *Why do many congregations sing "Children of the Heavenly Father" (LBW 474) when there is a Baptism? Sing the hymn. Discuss what the words really say.*
☐ *What is the purpose of the Sacrament of Holy Baptism?*
☐ *Bible verses for study:*
*Mark 16:15-16   Eph. 4:4-6   Matt. 3:13-17*
*Rom. 6:3-4*

THE SACRAMENT OF HOLY BAPTISM

**1. What is Baptism?**

Baptism is not water only, but it is water used together with God's Word and by his command.

**What is this Word?**

In Matthew 28 our Lord Jesus Christ says: *"Go therefore and make disciples of all nations, baptizing them in the name of the Father and of the Son and of the Holy Spirit."*

43

### What benefits does God give in Baptism?

As Jesus gave it to us, Baptism marks God's adoption of the Christian believer into the life of faith. This adoption is solely God's decision about us, not ours concerning God. That is why Lutherans and many other Christians baptize even the tiniest babies. Even infants can be adopted. The smallest children, like the most independent adults, can trust those who care for them.

In Baptism God adopts us as children and gives to each of us all that is most basic to life. In Baptism God forgives our sin, literally washing us clean of it, and opens to us a redeemed life as it was meant to be lived. In Baptism God grants the gift of a life that will not end in death. Another way of putting it is to say that in Baptism God gives us salvation. God saves us from sin and from death itself.

It is important to pay attention to what the passage from Mark 16 says and does not say. Jesus made it plain that Baptism is for saving and not for condemning. Baptism, commanded and instituted by Jesus, is intended to create faith in God in us out of our faithlessness. In remembrance of one's own Baptism, faith is made new again each day. That someone is not baptized does not mean that such a woman or man cannot be or will not be given the gift of salvation. For that, only God's Word and faith are needed, and God alone knows who the faithful are. Baptism *includes* rather than *excludes*, and the lack of Baptism does not preclude faith. But the question remains, "Why would anyone choose not to be baptized once God's promises are heard?"

☐ *What does God begin in us at the time of our Baptism?*
☐ *Why is it so difficult to believe that Christ gives all the gifts promised in Baptism?*
☐ *Bible verses for study:*
*1 Pet. 3:18-22  Rom. 8:28-30  John 14:18-21*

### 2. What benefits does God give in Baptism?

In Baptism God forgives sin, delivers from death and the devil, and gives everlasting salvation to all who believe what he has promised.

### What is God's promise?

In Mark 16 our Lord Jesus Christ says: *"He who believes and is baptized will be saved; but he who does not believe will be condemned."*

*How can water do such great things?* In this question and answer, Luther again emphasized that water without God's Word is only water. But used together with the Word of God, the water of Baptism creates faith and makes us alive in a way different and fuller than we might ever have imagined possible. Trust in this "visible word" of God is not a precondition for receiving the benefits of Baptism. God's Word through the work of the Holy Spirit creates faith and trust in us. We are therefore justified (made right with God) by God's own decision.

When you were baptized, in fact, you were literally regenerated or born again. That is what the apostle Paul was talking about in this startling passage from his letter to Titus when he calls Baptism "the washing of regeneration."

You have been baptized; that is, you have been justified. To be "justified" means that you are saved. Baptism is your entry into that kind of life and the assurance that at its end you will be ushered into an even fuller life when you and all who believe will be raised from the dead to enjoy life forever.

□ *How would you answer a person who asks if you have been born again?*
□ *If one could separate the Word from the water in Baptism, what would be the effect?*
□ *Bible verses for study:*
*John 3:1-8  1 Cor. 6:9-11  Psalm 139:13-18*

### 3. How can water do such great things?

It is not water that does these things, but God's Word with the water and our trust in this Word. Water by itself is only water, but with the Word of God it is a life-giving water which by grace gives the new birth through the Holy Spirit.

St. Paul writes in Titus 3: *"He saved us . . . in virtue of his own mercy, by the washing of regeneration and renewal in the Holy Spirit, which he poured out on us richly through Jesus Christ our Savior, so that we might be justified by his grace and become heirs in hope of eternal life. The saying is sure."*

**What does Baptism mean for daily living?** Luther kept the worst and the best about Baptism for this last question and answer. Perhaps this was because it is at once terribly frightening and wonderfully exhilarating. Following Paul, Luther taught that Baptism is an incorporation into the death and the resurrection of Jesus.

Stop to think about that for a moment. It is a very hard teaching. When babies, children, or adults are brought to Baptism, they are put to death, as Paul wrote in Romans 6:3-4. Through Baptism people die to their old sinful selves so that they may enter into the resurrection that waited for Jesus on the other side of that death. Baptism is the death of the old and resurrection to the new life in Christ.

That is why Luther insisted that Baptism is something to be renewed and experienced every day. Day after day Christians are called on to enter into the death of Jesus through repentance, the process of recognizing sin, sorrowing over it, and seeking God's forgiveness. Christians do this in the confidence that beyond repentance there waits resurrection, the experience of renewed life.

Christians can hold to this new life even amidst all the trouble, trials, pain, and death of this world. Baptism into Christ does not remove us from this world; indeed, we die to it. For Christians, life moves from death to birth, from repentance to renewal, from Baptism into the death of Christ, from a date remembered to participation in his resurrection on a day yet to come.

☐ *Why does repentance include feeling sorry for what was done?*
☐ *What effect does God's greatest gift of forgiveness have on your life?*
☐ *Bible verses for study:*
*Luke 19:1-10   Rom. 14:7-9   Eph. 4:17-24*

### 4. What does Baptism mean for daily living?

It means that our sinful self, with all its evil deeds and desires, should be drowned through daily repentance; and that day after day a new self should arise to live with God in righteousness and purity forever.

St. Paul writes in Romans 6: *"We were buried therefore with him by Baptism into death, so that as Christ was raised from the dead by the glory of the Father, we too might walk in newness of life."*

# For Reflection

**1.** Luther discussed both the promise on which Baptism is based and the benefits it offers. How would you summarize both?

**2.** Repentance is burial and forgiveness is rebirth according to Luther. How does the routine of your daily life reflect this conviction about the meaning and effects of Baptism?

**3.** If Baptism is God's act of adopting people into faith, what can you say to those who are baptized but appear to have fallen away from faith? What can you say to parents or friends of unbaptized infants or of young children who are not baptized?

# Our Prayers

The service of Holy Baptism in *Lutheran Book of Worship* (page 121) begins with the following declaration concerning Baptism.

> In Holy Baptism our gracious heavenly Father liberates us from sin and death by joining us to the death and resurrection of our Lord Jesus Christ. We are born children of a fallen humanity; in the waters of Baptism we are reborn children of God and inheritors of eternal life. By water and the Holy Spirit we are made members of the Church which is the body of Christ. As we live with him and with his people, we grow in faith, love, and obedience to the will of God.

Reflect aloud or silently on the significance of Baptism in your life. You may wish to use the hymn "All Who Believe and Are Baptized" (*LBW* 194) as a prayer to conclude these moments of meditation.

# Food For Travelers

**Luther's Small Catechism** flaunts it rather than hides it: The Christian way of life is rigorous and demanding. The Christian faith invites repentance and promises resurrection every day. Life on these terms is arduous. It consumes the resources of faith at an astonishing rate. It is no surprise, then, that weariness and doubt are familiar companions to Christians, and faithlessness and despair always lurk around them. No Christians evade these enemies completely, and some contend with them often. It requires a healthy and strong faith to contend with them. That is why many Christians will tell you that their faith needs regular nourishment.

For this reason Christians regularly gather with other believers to speak and hear the gospel—the message about the life and death and resurrection of Jesus. In doing so, they often talk of Baptism and remind themselves of the promises attached to this sacrament. When they are hungry for solid food, they come to a meal laid out for them by Jesus Christ himself, the Lord's Supper. Like a meal eaten by the side of the road, the Lord's Supper is food for travelers who are always on the way from repentance to resurrection, from death to birth.

Christians have many names for this meal. It is sometimes called the Sacrament of the Altar to emphasize the importance of Christ's sacrifice for our sin. More often it is referred to as Holy Communion to accent the intimate bond created between those who come to the meal and its host. In recent years, some Lutherans have begun to use the term *Eucharist*, a Greek term meaning "thanksgiving." The name for this sacrament most often used in the New Testament is the Lord's Supper. The name "Lord's Supper" identifies whose supper it is. It is the *Lord's* supper, not ours. It is a meal eaten in faith in God's promise to save.

**What is Holy Communion?** The New Testament teaches that on the night before he was put to death, Jesus paused during a meal with his followers and made a promise to them. Taking bread and a cup of wine into his hands, he gave this food and drink to his disciples and promised them that he would be with them in these things for all time to come.

As with the water of Baptism, bread and wine alone would be no more than ordinary food without the promise that in these ordinary things Jesus is really present to save. Christ's saving presence is there for us even if we should despise or not believe the promise of this meal. The Word and the promise of the Lord's Supper depend on God, not on our own ability to create what we think is faith or trust.

Once again, Christians can rely on the specific command of Christ to be present in this meal and on the promise he makes about it.

The promise has two parts. First, Jesus declares that he is indeed present. How he will be present he does not say, and speculation about that how usually creates more difficulties than it resolves. Second, Jesus indicates that he meets us in this meal for a definite purpose. He comes to this table to

## 1. What is Holy Communion?

Holy Communion is the body and blood of our Lord Jesus Christ given with bread and wine, instituted by Christ himself for us to eat and drink.

### Where do the Scriptures say this?

Matthew, Mark, Luke, and Paul say:

*Our Lord Jesus Christ, in the night in which he was betrayed, took bread; and when he had given thanks, he broke it and gave it to his disciples, saying, "Take, eat, this is my body, which is given for you; this do in remembrance of me."*

*After the same manner also he took the cup after supper, and when he had given thanks, he gave it to them, saying, "Drink of it, all of you; this cup is the new testament in my blood, which is shed for you, and for many, for the remission of sins; this do as often as you drink it, in remembrance of me."*

feed and nourish us in the faith that in his death he has won the forgiveness of our sins and the sure hope in the resurrection from the dead. When he said of both bread and wine, "This do in remembrance of me," he was not simply asking us to remember him, but he proclaimed clearly to us the saving events of his death and resurrection. As Paul wrote, in the Lord's Supper we "proclaim the Lord's death until he comes" (1 Corinthians 11:26b). Through reception of this meal, we receive the faith to believe and trust in God's promise of life and salvation.

☐ *What is the relationship of Holy Communion to Baptism?*
☐ *How can we be certain that Christ will be present with us in this meal?*
☐ *Bible verses for study:*
*Acts 2:37-42  1 Cor. 10:16-17  John 13:1-10*

**What benefits do we receive from this sacrament?** To make sure that you do not miss the point of Christ's promises, Luther asked the question as bluntly as he could: What good is this meal? What are its benefits?

Its benefits are not merely calories for your body, but the assurance of the forgiveness of sins, the thing most essential to life as it was meant to be lived. As Luther put it, only when your sins are forgiven can you know what it really is to live. The biblical word for that is *salvation*. Forgiven of your sins, you are called into action as a partner in the work of God to claim the whole world and your corner of it for life. You can be sure that there is nothing more you need. As Luther said in the Small Catechism, "For where there is forgiveness of sins, there is also life and salvation."

☐ *Why is it so difficult to accept the word of forgiveness in the Lord's Supper?*
☐ *How often do you think the Lord's Supper should be available? Why?*

---

**2. What benefits do we receive from this sacrament?**

The benefits of this sacrament are pointed out by the words, *"given and shed for you for the remission of sins."* These words assure us that in the sacrament we receive forgiveness of sins, life, and salvation. For where there is forgiveness of sins, there is also life and salvation.

☐ *Bible verses for study:*
*Psalm 51*     *Matt. 5:21-24*     *Eph. 2:1-10*

### How can eating and drinking do all this?

Like Luther's question about the water of Baptism, this one is designed to turn our attention from the elements of bread and wine and from the physical act of eating toward the promise attached to these things. It is not bread and wine alone that brings us nourishment in this meal; it is the promise of Jesus that makes this meal vital to Christian faith. It is meant for our hearts more than our stomachs because it is food for living faith.

Participation in the supper adds nothing to the faith already created when the message of Jesus' death and resurrection is heard with the ear and believed with the heart. The Lord's Supper, like the water of Baptism, is given to us to nourish and strengthen the faith that comes to us by the work of the Holy Spirit through the ear and lodges in our hearts. What is most important in this meal is not the eating or the drinking, but the announcement again and again of the promise made by Jesus to forgive our sins. To hammer this home, Luther was fond of quoting Augustine (A.D. 354–430) who said, "Believe and you have already eaten."

The Lord's Supper is meant to nourish your body and your faith, but the promise is more important than the food that it is. Our prayers of thanks and intercessions, an important part of Christian worship addressed to God, belong elsewhere in the service. The words of institution—"This is my body" and "This . . . is . . . my blood" and "for you and for many for the remission of sins"—are promises spoken by Jesus directly to us. They are the reason for our eating and drinking this nourishing food for travelers.

**3. How can eating and drinking do all this?**

It is not eating and drinking that does this, but the words, "given and shed for you for the remission of sins." These words, along with eating and drinking, are the main thing in the sacrament. And whoever believes these words has exactly what they say, forgiveness of sins.

□ *Why does such a simple thing as eating and drinking have such importance in our confession of faith?*
□ *What should our attitude be as we go to receive the Lord's Supper?*
□ *Bible verses for study:*
*Mark 2:1-12   2 Cor. 5:16-21   John 6:35-40 John 6:53-58*

## When is a person rightly prepared?

Christians do not take participation in the Lord's Supper lightly. By long tradition they prepare for this event by reflecting on its significance and spending time in prayer before they come to the table. Among some Christians it is customary to fast as a way of disciplined preparation for attendance at the Lord's Supper. Others regularly engage in self-examination and confession before coming to the table of the Lord. In the Small Catechism, Luther suggested that exercises like this may serve the good purpose of helping us prepare to take part in the Lord's Supper.

None of these exercises, however, make us worthy of the gifts we receive there. All that is asked of us is that we have "simply a believing heart." If we remember that it is God who creates the faith we need through hearing of the Word and receiving the Lord's Supper, we should not fear to come even when we feel that we have no faith. Christ calls us to this meal even when we feel unworthy, for it is the Word of God given in this meal that makes us worthy to receive it.

To wait until you feel especially holy or worthy is to ignore the very gifts that are given in the meal. Simply come, receive. God will do what is required.

□ *How do you know when you are worthy to receive this sacrament?*
□ *How do you respond when someone gives you a great gift? How do you respond when you receive the Lord's Supper?*
□ *Bible verses for study:*
*1 Cor. 11:27-32   Matt. 8:5-13   Eph. 2:1-10*

**4. When is a person rightly prepared to receive this sacrament?**

Fasting and other outward preparations serve a good purpose. However, that person is well prepared and worthy who believes these words, "given and shed for you for the remission of sins." But anyone who does not believe these words, or doubts them, is neither prepared nor worthy, for the words "for you" require simply a believing heart.

**1.** Describe for yourself or for another person inquiring about the Christian faith the benefits of participating in the Lord's Supper.

**2.** What did Augustine and Luther want to emphasize when they said, "Believe and you have already eaten"? (See page 51.)

**3.** In many congregations it is customary to use the Brief Order for Confession and Forgiveness (*LBW*, page 56) prior to the observance of the Lord's Supper. Do you think this practice is appropriate? Why would you recommend it for your congregation if it is not a regular part of the worship service?

## Our Prayers

Read and reflect on 1 Corinthians 11:27-32. You may wish to conclude with the following prayer.

> We do not presume to come to your table, O merciful Lord, trusting in our own righteousness, but in your manifold and great mercies. We are not worthy to gather up the crumbs under your table. But you are the same Lord whose property is always to have mercy. Grant us, therefore, gracious Lord, so to eat the flesh of your dear Son Jesus Christ, and so to drink his blood, that we may evermore dwell in him and he in us.
> (*LBW*, page 48)

# Going It
# Together

**Faith is** at once an intensely personal affair and, at the same time, a matter of concern for a whole community called the church. On the one hand, God saves one person at a time. On the other hand, when you enter into the life of faith, you become part of a community that makes that venture together. Think of the church as a choir. It could not make a sound without individual voices, but it is the voices blending together that make the choir. Christians do not go it alone. They go it together.

It is important not to lose sight of either the personal or the communal character of Christian faith. When you stake your life on faith, you enter into an intimate, direct relation with God. No one else can believe or trust God for you. No other human can give you faith and no community can have faith for you. No one can do that and no church or minister should pose as a necessary intermediary between you and God.

At the same time, one fruit of the experience of faith and one effect of Baptism is membership in a community of believers. Christians call that community the church. In our language *church* is an old word of unknown origin, but in the New Testament its meaning is clear. The church is the community of people who listen to the message

*A seven-year-old child knows what the church is, namely, holy believers and sheep who hear the voice of their Shepherd.*
*—Martin Luther*

55

of God and, through the work of the Holy Spirit, believe it. Martin Luther once summed it up very neatly in his own clear style. "What is the church?" he asked. He answered: "A seven-year-old-child knows what the church is, namely, holy believers and sheep who hear the voice of their Shepherd" (*BC* 315.2).

Luther went on to say that the church does not require unity or uniformity in forms of Christian worship, in the organization of the church, or in opinion on a variety of matters. Historically, Lutherans have often been narrow and even rigid in many of these things, but at their best they have also been remarkably creative and flexible in their expressions of Christian faith and life. Lutherans, in fact, understand Christians to be perfectly free in all these things—so long as they hear and hold to the message of God recorded in the Bible.

Some years after he published the Small Catechism, Luther turned to questions about life in the church in a large book called *On the Councils and the Church.* In this book, Luther set out a very simple explanation of the nature of the church. The church is known by seven characteristic marks: 1) the Word of God; 2) Baptism; 3) the Lord's Supper; 4) confession and absolution; 5) the ministry; 6) worship; and 7) suffering.

## The Seven Marks of the Church

**The Word of God.** If you are around Lutherans very long you will hear them talking endlessly about the Word of God. They may mean the Bible or they may be talking about the message of God written in the Bible that comes alive when people tell one another about it, hear it, and believe it. They may also refer to Jesus Christ himself whom the Bible calls the Word of God made flesh among us (John 1:1-14).

Another phrase Lutherans often use is "the gospel." By this word they mean the unconditional word of God that makes us

56

right with God. As Paul wrote, "For by grace you have been saved through faith, and this is not your own doing; it is the gift of God—not the result of works, so that no one may boast" (Ephesians 2:8-9).

The "Gospel," as Luther once said, "is a story about Christ, God's and David's Son, who died and was raised and is established as Lord. This is the Gospel in a nutshell" (*LW* 35:118).

It is the passing on of this story that creates the church. When people tell it, hear it, and believe it, they are the church. There is no more to it than that. That is the church "in a nutshell."

☐ *A "living word" makes things happen such as, "I love you." A "dead word" merely passes on information such as, "It is November." Is the Bible a "living word" or a "dead word"? Why?*
☐ *Bible verses for study:*
*John 1:1-14    Isa. 56:6-8    John 14:1-14*

**Baptism and the Lord's Supper.** Christians sometimes say that they are people who have been born again. Lutherans point to Baptism as the occasion of that new birth. It is the moment when their old selves were drowned, were put to death, and they were born again and made members of the church through the work of the Holy Spirit. For that reason, they regard Baptism as the actual presence of the church.

Lutherans believe that Baptism is for saving, not condemning. They do not say that those who are not baptized cannot be born again or belong to the church. This knowledge is a great source of comfort and strength to people who sometimes wonder if God cares for them or if they are truly a part of the church. As Luther put it, "Wherever you see this sign (or sacrament) you may know that the church, or the holy Christian people, must surely be present" (*LW* 41:151).

*Lutherans believe that Baptism is for saving, not condemning.*

The Lord's Supper testifies to the reality of the church in the same way. It is food for faith and a sign of the presence of the church. Where the promises of Jesus are spoken over bread and wine and where these gifts are received, there you may be sure that there is forgiveness of sin and the church.

☐ *Why do you think God comes to us through water, bread, and wine and not with pure power and might?*
☐ *What do the sacraments do that simple speech cannot always do?*
☐ *Bible verses for study:*
*Eph. 6:10-20    Matt. 18:20    Isa. 40:6-8*

**Confession and Absolution.** Jesus gave his disciples what he called the keys of the kingdom (see Matthew 18:18 and John 20:23) and said that they could lock the sins of one another or turn the key and set each other free with a word of forgiveness. Ever since, followers of Jesus have followed the practice of confessing their sin to God before one another and assuring one another of the forgiveness promised to them by Christ.

While it is good and fitting for Christians to confess to one another in private and to hear from each other's lips the promise of forgiveness, it has also been the practice of the church to do this in public as well. This exercise of the Office of the Keys is therefore another mark of the church that tells much about the faith and life of its people. That is also why Luther's Small Catechism has a section devoted to the Office of the Keys. (The Office of the Keys and Confession are printed on page 64 of this study book.)

☐ *Why does it help to confess your sins to another person?*
☐ *Why should we confess sins not known to us?*
☐ *Bible verses for study:*
*Matt. 18:15-20   Luke 15:11-24   Psalm 25*

**Ministry.** Because the church is a collection of a people gathered by God to hear God's saving word, it requires people to speak this word aloud. That is the function of the ministers of the church. The New Testament makes it clear that all Christians are charged with the duty of telling the story of God's saving decision in Jesus Christ to one another, to their families, and to people who have not yet heard it. As Lutherans often say, all Christians are in this sense ministers or priests of God.

But what about public gatherings? Who is to speak there? Luther talked about it this way in his book *On the Councils and the Church*. "The people as a whole cannot do these things, but must entrust or have them entrusted to one person. Otherwise, what would happen if everyone wanted to speak or to administer, and no one wanted to give way to the other?" (*LW* 41:154). In public, as in private, spoken words require a speaker. The sacraments require people to proclaim the promises of Jesus, to pour the water for washing, and to serve the food for eating. God, Lutherans teach, has ordered that the church always do these things, and so it is necessary for the church to call, by means of its own choosing, people to do these tasks in public.

By long tradition Lutherans call these servants *ministers*. Another favorite term for these workers, borrowed from sheep herding, is *pastor*, the one who takes care of the flock. Where ministers or pastors are at work speaking the Word of God and administering the Sacraments of Baptism and the Lord's Supper according to the teaching of the Scriptures, you may be sure the church is there and about its proper business.

☐ *Since we are ministers or "priests" to one another, what does this mean we should be doing?*
☐ *Bible verses for study:*
*1 Cor. 12:4-11  1 Cor. 12:12-31  Eph. 2:19-22*

**Worship.** Because Lutherans understand all Christians to be priests, they take it for granted that all of them will worship God daily. This worship happens by telling the story of the life and death and resurrection of Jesus in their homes and to other people whose lives touch theirs, by talking to God in prayer, and by speaking and singing the praise of God.

Lutherans also regularly gather on Sunday and other times as well to worship in public. Worship, beginning and ending in the Word of God, is for Lutherans their mission in the world—the telling of the Word of God to anyone who will listen. Telling the Christian story in reading Scripture and preaching, in Baptism and the Lord's Supper, and in regular prayer are the staples of Lutheran worship. Another regular part of worship is the giving of gifts of money for the work of the church in the world. In worship—in listening, confessing, forgiving, believing, giving, receiving, and praying—Christians rehearse and steep themselves in the most profound truths of their faith. They become aware, among other things, that hearers of the Word are also bearers and doers of it in the world.

☐ *How can regular worship with a community strengthen your faith?*
☐ *How can your worship strengthen others?*
☐ *Bible verses for study:*
*Acts 2:41-47     John 4:21-26     Rom. 6:1-5*

**Suffering.** If there is anything that can commend Christian faith to the skeptical or the wounded, it is its realism. Luther understood this well. In saying that suffering was an unmistakable mark of the church, he took the facts of life into account. Terrible things do happen to people. Humans do inflict horrible violence on each other. Natural terrors stalk all of us. Earthquakes kill by the thousands and cancer kills one by one.

There is, however, more to the notion that suffering is a mark of the church. Jesus, Christians say, was the Word of God become flesh. By that they mean that Jesus became fully human. He became flesh all the way and entered into all of the realities of human life, including death. When he died, nailed to a cross, brutalized and bleeding, he endured human suffering at its worst.

The community of believers that calls Jesus "Lord," Luther taught, can expect the same contempt and even violence at the hands of the world. As Luther put it, Christians can expect "inward sadness, timidity, fear, outward poverty, contempt, illness, and weakness" to come with faith. Lutherans know that a part of the church's calling in the world is to suffer. If that were all there is to Christian faith, it would be both tragic and heroic but nothing more. There is, however, much more to the Christian trust in God.

Three days after Jesus died, God raised him from the dead and promised that all who put their trust in him would also be raised from the dead one day in the future. That is an unshakable article of faith for Christians. They believe that entering into the suffering of Christ is a part of their calling as Christians, a result of their Baptism into his death. At the same time, they claim a part in his resurrection as well. It is their confidence in the resurrection of Christ and their hope in a future like his for themselves that give Christians the honest courage to face suffering as it really is, to remove it where they can, and to confide it to God where they cannot. It is a profoundly honest faith that Christians hold and one they can boldly commend to the world.

☐ *How can knowing that one is baptized bring comfort during times of suffering?*
☐ *Bible verses for study:*
*1 Pet. 4:12-19     Psalm 22     Job 42:1-6*

*Lutherans know that a part of the church's calling is to suffer the facts of life and the trials of faithfulness.*

**In conclusion,** the Christian faith is so bold a venture that Christians find themselves grateful that they do not undertake it alone. As members of the church they are glad to go it together, knowing that only a good and a generous God could make a community so marvelous out of such an unlikely gaggle of humanity as the Christian

church is. That is perhaps why Lutherans often remember best these lines from the explanation of the Third Article of the Apostles' Creed in the Small Catechism:

> I believe that I cannot by my own understanding or effort believe in Jesus Christ my Lord, or come to him. But the Holy Spirit has called me through the Gospel, enlightened me with his gifts, and sanctified and kept me in true faith. In the same way he calls, gathers, enlightens, and sanctifies the whole Christian church on earth, and keeps it united with Jesus Christ in the one true faith. In this Christian church day after day he fully forgives my sins and the sins of all believers. On the last day he will raise me and all the dead and give me and all believers in Christ eternal life. This is most certainly true.

**1.** Consider the seven marks of the church as Luther identified them. Is there anything left out? Are there any that you think do not belong?

**2.** Lutherans understand the church to be free to adopt a variety of forms and practices in different times and places. How does Luther's understanding of the church help to make decisions about such things?

**3.** What does it mean to say that hearing the word also involves bearing the word and doing the word? Read 1 Peter 2:9-10 and James 1:22-25 as you consider this.

**Our Prayers**

Read aloud the Prayer of the Church on pages 52-53 of *Lutheran Book of Worship.* Think about the marks of the church and its involvement with the world of which it is a part.

# THE OFFICE OF THE KEYS AND CONFESSION

## What is the "Office of the Keys"?

It is that authority which Christ gave to his church to forgive the sins of those who repent and to declare to those who do not repent that their sins are not forgiven.

## What are the words of Christ?

Our Lord Jesus Christ said to his disciples: "Receive the Holy Spirit. If you forgive the sins of any, they are forgiven; if you retain the sins of any they are retained." —John 20:23

"Truly, I say to you, whatever you bind on earth shall be bound in heaven, and whatever you loose on earth shall be loosed in heaven." —Matthew 18:18

CONFESSION

## What is private confession?

Private confession has two parts. First, we make a personal confession of sins to the pastor, and then we receive absolution, which means forgiveness as from God himself. This absolution we should not doubt, but firmly believe that

thereby our sins are forgiven before God in heaven.

## What sins should we confess?

Before God we should confess that we are guilty of all sins, even those which are not known to us, as we do in the Lord's Prayer. But in private confession, as before the pastor, we should confess only those sins which trouble us in heart and mind.

## What are such sins?

We can examine our everyday life according to the Ten Commandments—for example, how we act toward father or mother, son or daughter, husband or wife, or toward the people with whom we work, and so on. We may ask ourselves whether we have been disobedient or unfaithful, bad-tempered or dishonest, or whether we have hurt anyone by word or deed.

## How might we confess our sins privately?

We may say that we wish to confess our sins and to receive absolution in God's name. We may begin by saying, "I, a poor sinner, confess

before God that I am guilty of many sins." Then we should name the sins that trouble us. We may close the confession with the words, "I repent of all these sins and pray for mercy. I promise to do better with God's help."

## What if we are not troubled by any special sins?

We should not torture ourselves with imaginary sins. If we cannot think of any sins to confess (which would hardly ever happen), we need not name any in particular, but may receive absolution because we have already made a general confession to God.

## How may we be assured of forgiveness?

The pastor may pronounce the absolution by saying, "By the authority of our Lord Jesus Christ I forgive you your sins in the name of the Father and of the Son and of the Holy Spirit. Amen."

Those who are heavily burdened in conscience the pastor may comfort and encourage with further assurances from God's Word.